Imran batting for Oxford University in 1974.

2 The team captain

In 1982,
Imran was made captain of the Pakistan team.
He made them
one of the world's greatest teams.

These were the best times for Imran.
Before him, the Pakistan team
had been just a group of players.
Many of them were very good,
but they played just for themselves.
Imran made them into a team.

Test matches last for five days,
and you need a strong captain
to keep the team together.
Imran did that.
He made the players play at their best
for all of the match,
and to play for the team.

Contents

1 The superstar

Imagine you were a sports star.
Imagine you were the captain
of your country's team.

Imagine you were a hero
to all the people in your country.

And then imagine
you had a beautiful young wife,
who was the daughter
of one of the richest men in the world.

And then imagine
that you were an important person
in your country,
and that people were saying
you would be the next prime minister.

It sounds impossible, doesn't it?
It could only happen in a film,
not in real life.
But for Imran Khan all these things are true,
and many more as well.

He was born in 1952
in Lahore in Pakistan.
His family was well off,
and he began to learn cricket
when he was still very young.

He had two cousins.
Both played cricket for Pakistan.

He was sent to England,
and played cricket for Oxford University.
People started to notice him.
They said he would be a great cricketer.

In 1971, he played for Pakistan
for the first time.
It was a test match against England,
and it was played in Birmingham.
Imran did not play well,
but it was the first of his many matches
for Pakistan.

Imran playing for Pakistan in 1971.

Imran was an 'all-rounder',
good at batting and bowling.
He was a powerful batsman,
and hit the ball very hard.
He could score a lot of runs very quickly.

He was also a very fast bowler.
At his best,
he was the fastest bowler in the world.
Batsmen were all afraid of him.
He always opened the bowling for Pakistan.

But perhaps the best thing about Imran
was that he made other players play better.

They looked up to him.
They listened to what he said,
and in this way he helped them play
the very best cricket they could.

While Imran was captain,
Pakistan beat every other cricketing country
in the world.

In 1982, they beat England away,
and Imran took 21 wickets in three matches.

Their best win was over Australia
at home in Pakistan.
They beat them three times in a row.

Imran became the most famous man
in Pakistan.
Crowds mobbed him everywhere he went.
This was a great shock to Imran.
No cricketer had been so popular before.
He was not expecting it.
It could have gone to his head.
But his family helped him.
His father told him
that all his success was a gift from God.
'All honour and disgrace,' says the Quran,
'is in the hands of Allah.'

Imran bowling for Pakistan in 1982.

Cricket became the most popular sport
in Pakistan.
Even today in all the streets
in all the towns
you see young boys playing cricket.
All of them trying to be a better batsman
or a better bowler,
and all of them dreaming
of being like Imran Khan.

If the boys liked Imran for his cricket,
the girls liked him
for his dark, good looks
and dashing style.

He was like a film star.
And his life was like a film star's.

He was seen in all the most fashionable places –
at an all-night club in London,
or skiing in the mountains,
or in Hollywood.
He was a friend of the rich and famous,
and there were always
lots of pretty girls around him.

But then it all ended!

3 Rich and famous

Bowling fast for a long time is very hard.
Bowling very fast is even harder.
It puts a special strain
on the joints in the leg.
A fast bowler has to be very fit,
otherwise he will collapse.
Imran was very fit,
but the strain of bowling
hour after hour,
day after day,
was too much.

In 1985, his knees began to give way.
Some days he could hardly walk,
let alone bowl.
Imran struggled on,
trying to bowl as fast as ever.
Finally the doctors said he must stop.
Otherwise he might never walk again.

It was a bitter blow for Imran.
He didn't want to talk to anyone.

He went off by himself on camping trips
to the mountains.
He spent weeks at a time in the wildest
and most remote parts of Pakistan.
And there he learnt to love the country
and the people in it.

And he also saw the poverty.

He saw how some people could not afford
proper food, or shelter, or clothing,
while the rich lived easily.
He saw how money went into the wrong pockets
while the poor starved.
And he saw how people died from simple illnesses
because their families
could not afford the right medicines.

And then his mother died of cancer.

Imran vowed then that he would build
a cancer hospital for the people of Pakistan.

He travelled the country
to raise money for the hospital.
Wherever he went,
crowds gathered round him.
They pushed banknotes into his hands,
even the poorest.

In 45 days Imran raised $4m.

To the people of Pakistan,
Imran wasn't just a star,
he was a saint as well.

And then in 1992
he agreed to play cricket again.
He captained Pakistan in the World Cup,
and they won!

It was unbelievable!
It seemed
that he could do anything!

He was like a god!

But no-one can be as popular as Imran
without making enemies!

Pakistan won the World Cup in 1992. Imran was the captain of the winning team.

In 1995, he married Jemima Goldsmith.
It was the wedding of the year.
She is the daughter of Sir James Goldsmith,
one of the world's richest men.
She is a friend of Princess Di.
Everyone was there,
and the wedding was in all the newspapers
and in all magazines
and on television.

All this made many people angry.
They said Imran had forgotten
he was from Pakistan.
They said that he was a hypocrite,
and didn't care about the people.
They said, 'Remember the night clubs,
and the parties, and the girls!'
They even said
he was not really a very good cricketer –
his team-mates called him 'Im the dim'!

And they said that Jemima was just a silly girl,
and she would not be a good wife.

They were wrong about Jemima.
She has tried hard to change her ways,
and fit in with the people of Pakistan.

Were they wrong about Imran?

Imran and Jemima.

4 The politician

Imran didn't just want to be a star.
He wanted to do more with his life.
He loved his country,
and he thought it was in a mess.
The people were poor, and were suffering.
Nothing seemed to work properly.

Imran began to make speeches
about the poverty,
and attacked the rich people
who did nothing about it.

He tried to make people
proud of their country,
and proud of their religion,
and proud of their culture.
He started to wear
the traditional clothes of Pakistan –
the *shalwar kameez* –
the long shirt and loose trousers.

Imran and Jemima wear traditional clothes most of the time.

This made him more enemies –
powerful enemies who thought
he was a danger to their power.

Imran began to receive threatening letters.
They told him not to carry on
with the hospital.

They said if he did so,
his life would be in danger.

And not only his life,
but also Jemima's and their unborn child's.

Imran carried on regardless.

In 1996, the hospital opened, in Lahore.
All the press and television were there.
It was a happy moment for Imran.
At last he could do some good for people.

Shortly after the hospital opened,
Princess Di came to stay
with Imran and Jemima.
Imran went to show her round the hospital.

Just before they arrived,
the hospital was blown apart by a huge bomb.
Six people died,
and forty were injured.

No-one knows who put the bomb there,
but everyone can guess
who it was meant for.

Imran was deeply shocked by the bomb.
He said,
'How could anyone do that?'
'How could anyone bomb a hospital
that was doing so much good?'
He was so upset by the bomb,
that he lost his temper with a reporter,
and hit him.

Imran said he was sorry,
but it shows why the papers in Pakistan
often write unkind things about Imran.

The bomb made Imran realise
how hard it would be
to change things in Pakistan,
and it made him try harder.

He started a political party,
called the Justice Party.
He hoped to win power,
so he could start to bring justice
to the poor people of Pakistan,
and fight corruption at the top.

But just as he was about to start work,
he had a summons,
to appear in court in London.

Imran has come a long way from his playboy days. He has started his own political party and a cancer hospital.

5 The court case

Ian Botham is one of the best-known cricketers
in the world.
He thought he had a case against Imran.
He thought that Imran had insulted him,
and had called him a cheat and a racist.
Imran said it wasn't true,
it was a misunderstanding,
and he hadn't said any of those things.
And in any case he had already offered
to say in public that he was sorry
for any misunderstanding Ian may have had.

But this was not enough for Ian.
He insisted the case went ahead,
and sued Imran for damages.

It was on television night after night.
It was all about whether Ian had cheated
in a cricket match,
by tampering with the ball.
Ian said that he had not cheated,
but that Imran said he had.
Imran said he hadn't said that at all.

In the end the case was thrown out,
and Imran was innocent.
But he was sad about it.
He had liked and respected Ian Botham.
And the court case had stopped him doing
what he wanted to do –
helping the people of Pakistan.

As soon as the case was over,
Imran hurried back to Pakistan.
The country was in crisis.
The President had been arrested,
and new elections called.
And now Imran and Jemima
had a baby son to care for as well.

Imran threw himself into the elections.
He wanted people to vote for the Justice Party,
and make him Prime Minister.

But then he had to face another court case.

Sita White is an heiress,
the daughter of Lord White.
She said that Imran was the father
of her daughter who was born in 1992.
What's more she said that
when Imran found out
the baby was going to be a girl,
he wanted her to get rid of her.

Imran denied it all.
He said it was all lies
put about by his enemies.
But he refused to have a blood test
to show whether he was the father or not.

The court ruled that Imran was the father.
But even before the verdict,
the people had decided.

February 6 1997 was election day in Pakistan.

When all the votes were counted,
it was seen that Imran's party, the Justice Party,
had not won a single seat!

The people's verdict was against him!

Imran is working hard to be accepted in Pakistan.

1997 was a hard year for Imran –
first the election and then the court case –
but he admits it has been harder for Jemima.
Her father died,
and then her great friend, Princess Di,
was killed in the famous car crash.
Imran being away so much
has put a great strain on the family.

So perhaps for Imran Khan,
the man who seemed to have everything,
life is no longer just a game of cricket.